THE POWER OF VISIONS AND DREAMS

Emile Austin

 Unless otherwise identified, Scripture quotations are taken from the Holy Bible, New Living Translation, copyright 1996, 2004. Scripture quotations marked AMP are taken from the Amplified Bible, copyright 1954, 1958, 1962, 1965, 1978 by The Lockman Foundation. Scripture quotations marked NIV are taken from the New International Version, copyright 1973, 1978, 1984, 2011. Scripture quotations marked NKJV are taken from the New King James Version, copyright 1982. Scripture quotations marked KJV are taken from the King James Version, copyright 1972 by Thomas Nelson Publishers. Scripture quotations marked NASB are taken from the New American Standard Version, copyright 1960, 1962, 1963, 1968, 1995. Please note Quality-rich eServices editing style capitalises certain pronouns and words used in reference to the Almighty God, and this may differ from other editors. Take note that the name devil or Satan is not capitalised and other related names.

Edited by qualityrichservices@gmail.com

Cover design by: Andrew Austin

ISBN Paperback: 978-1-0687417-0-8

For worldwide Distribution, Printed on Amazon

DEDICATION

I would like to dedicate this book to the loyal members of our local church, The Lighthouse Christian Ministries, Stratford, London who have been co-labourers with me from the beginning. The vision of trying to reach our community of over two hundred thousand people with the gospel of the Lord Jesus Christ was an extremely ambitious one, especially by a group of six largely young people who had no experience whatsoever of starting a church. However, they believed in the vision; they nurtured the vision; they embraced the vision and committed themselves to God first of all; and with His help, did everything within their power to seek to bring that vision to pass.

As a result, and some forty years later, there is now a thriving multicultural church in the East of our capital city, that by the grace of God, has not only developed leaders who have gone on to start ministries of their own both nationally and internationally, but even more importantly, after all these years, the vision of expanding the Kingdom of God is still alive in their hearts.

ACKNOWLEDGEMENT

To my Lord and Saviour - Jesus Christ – thanks for the grace You have given me to write this book.

To my "Little Big Sister" - Monica – thanks for your encouragement, your inspiration and your support. You have inspired me to put this first touch of paint on this literary canvas.

To my dear wife – Ann - whose love and zest for life has made our marriage a series of adventures. Thank you.

To my church family and well-wishers - I want to acknowledge you for sewing into my life throughout the years. Thank you.

TABLE OF CONTENTS

INTRODUCTION

Throughout this book, *The Power of Visions and Dreams,* we will be delving into the significance of dreams and visions, as vehicles first of all, for fulfilling God's purpose for our lives; and secondly, for our individual personal growth. We will uncover practical insights and timeless truths to awaken the latent potential within each dream and vision.

Join me on this transformative journey, where the veil between the seen and the unseen is lifted, and the power of dreams and visions becomes a tangible reality in our lives.

As the prophet Habakkuk proclaimed, *"Write down the revelation and make it plain on tablets so that a herald may run with it. For the revelation awaits an appointed time; it speaks of the end and will not prove false. Though it lingers, wait for it; it will certainly come and will not delay"* (Habakkuk 2:2-3, NIV)

May this journey ignite a fervent passion within us to embrace the fullness of God's very own dreams and visions for our lives and unlock the boundless potential that lies dormant within our spirits.

*"Write the **vision** and **make it plain UPON TABLES that** he may run that reads it".*

- *Habakkuk 2:2* (KJV)

*"Where there is no vision, **THE PEOPLE PERISH,** but he that keeps the law, happy is he".*

- *Proverbs 29:18* (NKJV

CHAPTER 1

THE MIRACULOUS POSSIBILITIES OF VISIONS AND DREAMS

All of life as we know it is the result of a vision. It is the result of God's very own vision. He thought about all of creation from eternity past; not only of this earth of ours, but of all the millions of galaxies and stars the scientists inform us exists. He saw how every one of those galaxies was going to function and what role they would play in His grand purpose in the universe. He thought about all of this, even before a single molecule was ever spoken into existence. He also thought of all the discoveries and the advances that mankind would make throughout the successive ages and structured all of this into creation. He thought about every single detail of this amazing and wonderful world of ours, millennia before they ever existed; and at the right time, He spoke everything He thought about into existence. Creation then is the expression of God's amazing vision.

Equally so, everything that we see in life today, from the ancient pyramids in Egypt that still baffles modern man as to how they were ever built; to the present skyscrapers scattered across the major cities of our world; some of which are so high that they seem to protrude through the clouds. All these came about from somebody's thoughts, dreams, or visions. All are the results of the thought process of someone's mind. Think of all the amazing scientific inventions that have been a blessing to mankind and have transformed human life on this spinning ball we humans call home; the great works of art or the musical masterpieces that have often left us speechless at their genius; someone, somewhere conceived it, thought about the possibility of it and in the end, brought it into existence. None of it came by accident.

So, therefore, the most powerful things in life are not the things that we can see, but the things we cannot see. Because all that we can see, and even some of what we cannot see, came from something that we cannot see, from the human mind or the human spirit. So, as we have said before, even the very universe itself, the scripture tells us, was the result of God's reasoning. As the Bible so clearly states in the Book of Hebrews 3:11 (KJV), *"By faith we understand that the universe was created by the word of God, so that what is seen was not made out of things that are visible"*. How incredible! This visible and invisible amazing world of ours, with all its wonder and beauty, came into being from the invisible world of God's mind.

That is why when we look at the splendour of creation and these amazing and complex designs that we see at every level of life, as well as the breathtaking order that governs creation, have to admit that there is more than sufficient evidence to convince us that all this could not have happened by chance. Some mind somewhere has conceived and constructed all of this. So, in this book, I will seek to provide a comprehensive exploration of the immense wealth and unparalleled power that comes with having visions and dreams.

AN AMAZING SCRIPTURE

In what I believe to be one of the greatest passages in the entire scriptures, is found an amazing statement that God made about the staggering capability of the human imagination. I want us to look at this scripture later. But here in Genesis 9:7, God gave a very specific and clear command to that small family that survived the flood; *"Be fruitful and multiply and repopulate the earth"*. (NLT)

This command, of course, extended to Noah's descendants which would make up the next generation. However, contrary to God's specific command, the scripture tells us of that generation's rebellious response to God's clear instruction. "*Come,*" they said, *"let us build for ourselves a city with a tower that reaches to the heavens; that we may make a name for ourselves and not be scattered over the face of all the earth" Genesis 11:4 (BSB).* They had discussed it, agreed and decided together to do the very opposite of what God had commanded them. They were completely united in their rebellious purpose; and even though this plan was contrary to what God had intended, with this kind of mindset, surprisingly, their building programme was extremely successful. So successful in fact that it actually attracted God's attention and provoked an almost immediate response from Him.

The Bible says that "*the Lord came down to see the city and the tower that the sons of men had built*". God's response to this building program; however, showed exactly where His main concerns were. It was not so much with the tower itself or even the city, as amazing and audacious as these were. No, it was rather **the way that the people were thinking** that concerned Him. Now, listen to the amazing scripture that we referred to earlier. "And *the LORD said, Behold,* ***the people is one****, and* ***they have all***

one language; *and this they begin to do:* ***and now nothing will be restrained from them,*** *WHICH THEY HAVE IMAGINED TO DO".* Genesis 11:6 (KJV) How amazing is this?

This staggering statement was not the result of their own assessment of themselves. It was not even the angel's assessment of them. No, this was God's very own assessment of His own creation. These were His creatures He had created in His very own image and likeness. He therefore is the One, who more than anyone else, knows the capability of His creation. This was His verdict on their newly discovered capability, even though, it was not clear whether they themselves realised that they had discovered something miraculous. This indicates that as human beings, there are limitless possibilities that lie latent within us; capabilities that most times we are unaware of. *"Nothing shall be restrained from them or be impossible unto them which they have imagined or dreamed to do,"* declared the Creator God about His rebellious subjects. Genesis 11:6B (KJV).

Has it occurred to us that these new capabilities the Lord declared they had stumbled upon are some of the very same statements that the scripture says about God Himself? Luke 1:37 (KJV) states; *"with God, nothing shall be impossible."* Mark 10:27 (KJV), *"with God, all things are possible."*

The interesting implication about this is that; **as long as we can conceive something, or dream about it and work together with like-minded folks, nothing, God Himself states, will be impossible to achieve.** Does this not blow your mind? Does this not show that there are possibilities that we, as God's creation, are capable of that we have still not yet discovered? And who the scriptures were talking about here were not God-fearing, righteous living followers of Jehovah. No, these were men in their fallen state; and at that time, were active in doing the very opposite of what He had explicitly commanded them. Now if God can say this about the capability of men who were in open rebellion against His directives, what about God's children whom He has chosen to carry His God-given visions and dreams?

We can clearly see the truth of this capability God highlighted then, even in our day, as scientists keep pushing the boundaries of science further and further in each generation, way beyond what man has in the past thought possible.

Of course, we are not implying that man is in any way equal to God, but the question is, are there things about man's capacity and capability that we have not yet discovered? If the spirit of man is the receptacle where we receive God's visions and dreams for ourselves and the world, what then are we capable of if we are able to dream God's dreams and receive His visions?

"All things are possible to him that believes".

- *Mark 9:23 (NKJV)*

CHAPTER 2

WHAT IS A VISION?

So far, we have been talking about the importance of having a vision, but now, the million-dollar question. What exactly is a vision? How do we get one? Many people, when they hear about having a vision or a dream, sometimes are not clear about what this really means. They think they have to fall into some trance-like state or have some special spiritual experience like the Apostle Paul on the Damascus Road before they can say they have a vision. Or even like the Apostle Peter, who whilst praying on the housetop, saw in a vision this sheet come down from heaven before him with all the various beasts on it, accompanied by the voice of God instructing him what to do.

Yes, those are exceptional cases where God supernaturally reveals His purpose to you. I would dare to say however that this is the exception, not the rule; at least, not necessarily what the Bible is talking about in the scriptures we are exploring. It would be wonderful if we all could experience these kinds of supernatural experiences all the time. However, the majority of us rarely do experience this.

The word vision in this passage is translated from a root word, ***"Chazon,"*** which to me seems to have three facets to its meaning.

1. The **act of seeing** or **the ability to see.**
2. Then the **actual thing seen** whether physical or mental.
3. *Then interestingly, the Oracle, or an oracle* **...** *a place at which Divine advice or prophecy was sought.* This point is vitally important as *it speaks of a person or a thing regarded as* ***an infallible authority on something.*** Of course, if you are a child of God, you know this to be the Word of God. This is the only infallible thing we have in this world.

So, to summarize; having a vision is first of all, **having the spiritual or the mental ability to see.** Then secondly, ***seeing the actual thing that you are envisioning or being shown;*** whether it relates to the Kingdom of God; your church; your ministry; your situation or your life.

THE ABILITY TO SEE

How important is it to be able to see? It is absolutely essential! Just ask a person without sight, or just imagine what life would be like if you could not see! You cannot enjoy all the wonderful things you hear people say, as you would love to. A person who cannot see has a quality of life vastly different from a person who can see. You can try to describe the beauty and the glory of the sun or the beauty of some wonderful landscape to a blind person and it will not mean the same thing to them as it does to you. If you are without sight, in many cases, very sadly, some people end up begging for a living. Jesus says that if the blind leads the blind, both will fall into the ditch. This is what it is like without our natural sight. Let me say that spiritually, it is even more essential that we can see into the spiritual realm. It is so essential that God Himself quite often tests His prophets, firstly to see that they have the ability to see.

Then secondly, He tests them to make sure that they are seeing the vision or what is being shown to them clearly and correctly. In Jeremiah 1:11-12, the scripture states, *"Moreover, the word of the Lord came unto me saying, Jeremiah, WHAT DO YOU SEE?"*

If we automatically saw correctly what God is showing us, then why should God be asking Jeremiah what he was seeing when God Himself was the one who was giving him and showing Jeremiah this vision? We would assume that because God is the one who was showing him this vision, there would be no question or doubt that he would automatically see it and see it correctly. However, that is not the case according to this scripture. Even though God shows us something, it does not mean that we always see it correctly or understand it correctly. Consequently, He has to take steps to find out first of all if we are seeing the vision as He is showing it to us— Jeremiah's response satisfied the Lord that he was indeed seeing the vision correctly. *"And I said, I see a rod of almond tree. Then said the Lord unto me, THOU HAST WELL SEEN".*

See that? When Jeremiah's declaration demonstrated to God that Jeremiah was seeing what he was being shown correctly, then the Lord proceeded to explain to Jeremiah what his vision meant. Amazing.

Sometimes, I wonder just how many of us as leaders are really seeing properly. God shows us something and we run ahead with the first impression, simply by being carried away with the experience of being shown something. However, many times we are still unclear about what He is showing us. We see the Lord doing the same thing to the prophet Amos in chapter 7:7-8 of his book, testing and checking to see exactly what he was seeing. *"Thus, He showed me; and behold the Lord stood upon a wall by a plumb line, with a plumb line in His hand. And the Lord said unto me, AMOS, WHAT SEEST THOU? And I said a plumb line…* then the Lord proceeded to explain what he had seen."

We see the same thing also in Zechariah 4:2 (KJV), *"And the angel that talked with me came again and waked me as a man that is wakened out of his sleep. And he said unto me. WHAT SEEST THOU?"* Again, after the prophet explained what he saw and what he understood of what he saw, **then the angel proceeded to explain to him the meaning of the vision.**

Now, tell me, in the light of these scriptures, does it seem to you that being able to see clearly is important to God? Well, He has asked three different prophets the very same thing, so what do you think? You bet He thinks it is important! Let me say it again. It is so essential that as Christians, people of God and leaders **we not only have the ability to see, but most importantly, we need to be able to see clearly what we are being shown.**

Sometimes we can be like that blind man whom Jesus healed in Mark 8:24 (KJV). The Bible says, Jesus led this man out of the town, then touched his eyes and then *ASKED HIM WHAT HE SAW*. Notice, Jesus did not ask him *if he could see,* but rather *WHAT* he saw. If Jesus asked him if he could see anything, he could have answered "yes", but gone away with defective vision. However, it was important to Jesus to hear what this poor blind man saw, **even after having received a miracle from Jesus Himself.** He replied, *"I see men as trees walking."* Yes, he got a miraculous touch, but not enough to make him complete and be able to see as clearly and properly as he should. Do we not see a message in this miracle? A very clear one. He was not seeing clearly enough EVEN THOUGH HE HAD A TOUCH FROM JESUS and so he needed another touch. May I say as leaders, we cannot minister on the level of just one touch sometimes. The early disciples were refilled with the Holy Spirit on numerous occasions way after that first outpouring on the Day of Pentecost.

What really scares me, and I don't mind telling you, is this. Becoming like what Jesus called the Pharisees in Matthew 23:16 and 24, **blind guides. These Pharisees were guiding people, but they did not see that they could not see.** Imagine that, not being able to see that you cannot see. Yes, having visions and dreams are essential; so essential that God promised that having visions and dreams was going to be ONE OF THE FIRST CONSEQUENCE of the baptism of the Holy Ghost. Joel 2:28 (KJV) states... *Your young men shall see visions; your old men shall dream dreams."*

IN THE BUSINESS WORLD

In the business world, they will teach you that having a vision is the very first step in strategic planning to develop and grow your business. No company will be successful without a vision. If by chance they become successful, they will not be able to maintain that success without a vision. That is why no banks will even let you through their doors, much less lend you a penny for your proposed business without a business plan (or a vision) for that business.

A vision for your business is the picture and the plan you have in your head of what you want that business to become or what you think it is capable of becoming.

Do you know when a bank lends you a million or two million pounds for your business, they estimate that the vision you have given them for that business is far more valuable than that? That is why they are prepared to invest in your business. **This tells me that in every vision, there are more than enough resources to**

service that vision. So, whether it is a business, a church, your ministry, your home, your life, or your marriage, you must have a vision for it, and that vision is far more valuable than you can imagine.

It is said that there is more than enough wealth in a single grain of corn to feed the entire world. Just plant that one grain of corn and when it bears fruit, just repeat the process of replanting the seeds that it bears. Eventually, you will have enough grain to feed the entire world. Also, just imagine all the financial wealth that that single grain of corn will also produce! There are unimaginable resources that is contained in every vision. However, we must have the ability to see this.

THE DANGER OF NOT HAVING VISION

So far, we have been looking at the positive aspects of having visions and dreams. However, there is another side to this; this is the danger of having no visions or dreams. The Book of Proverbs tells us the tragic consequence of this: *"Where there is NO VISION THE PEOPLE PERISH."* An amazing but true statement. We only have to look all around us today to see that this is so.

According to *Strong's Analytical Concordance*, the word *perish* in Proverbs 29:18 is translated from the Hebrew word, *"Para,"* which means; *"to become loose", "exposed," "become uncovered or naked," "to go backwards."* Isn't that incredible? A lack of vision leaves people *uncovered, naked, and exposed, which causes them to go backwards.* Even without this scripture telling us this, we can see this clearly in our world today by the multitude of visionless lives perishing right before our eyes, yet all full of amazing potential. So, it is not the potential or the capability that these lives lack, it is the vision they do not possess.

Some modern translation of this passage says, that without a vision, people *"cast off restraints."* In other words, they live anyhow. There is no sense of purpose in their lives; no sense of destiny; they just live for the moment, reacting to whatsoever things the winds of life happen to blow across their lives from moment to moment. Of course, when one lives like that, casting off all restraints, we know, it always leads to one destination and that is destruction.

These are the negative results of not having a vision or a dream. Can you see the irony of it? Creatures who God has created in His image and likeness for a purpose, to fulfil that purpose, to be a blessing to their world, wind up living as though there is no reason for their existence. Your vision is meant to not only inspire and motivate you but also to keep your life within the constraints of the vision, which will eventually direct you to your destination. This is part of the price one has to pay when you have a vision. The fact is every vision has a cost factor and the first person it makes a demand upon to pay that cost is the one who has the vision. This price is being disciplined enough to live within the constraints of the vision. But where there is no vision, the people cast off constraints.

So, when it comes to the Kingdom of God, *it is having the ability to see God's plans for His Kingdom and for this world. It is also to see what is His specific plan for your life in that Kingdom. It is having the ability to see things as God sees them, from His standpoint, His perspective.* You know, it is one thing to see life from your perspective only, but looking at the same life from God's perspective is totally and completely different.

How many lives have this world thrown away as no good? Social rejects, moral and economic failures, but whom God collects, He completely changes and transforms them. He then turns around and sends these same people right back to be a blessing to those very communities who rejected them in the first place.

I am reminded of the men in the Old Testament who joined themselves to David whilst he was running from

King Saul. The Bible says in 1 Samuel 22:1-2 (NKJV), *"David departed from there and escaped to the cave of Adullam. And when his brothers and all his father's house heard it, they went down there to him;* ***and everyone who was in distress****, and* ***everyone who was in debt****, and everyone who was* **bitter in soul**, *(or discontented) gathered to him. And he became commander over them. And there were with him about four hundred men."*

To me, this is the ultimate picture of what being a failure looks like. These were failures on every level; distressed, discontented, and indebted. This was a group of people without a vision. These are not the type of people who you would naturally select if you were thinking of building a kingdom. Yet, these were the kinds of people whom God gave to David – all social outcasts. Later in our study, however, we will come back to these men and have a closer look at them and their amazing achievements after they received a vision.

"Whenever God wants to change the world, He gives someone a great vision".

Emile Austin

CHAPTER 3

THE GIFT OF VISIONS AND DREAMS

We have the very inspirational and popular scripture that preachers frequently quote and preach from in the Book of Joel 2:28 (ESV), *"And it shall come to pass afterward, that I will pour out my Spirit upon all flesh; and your sons and your daughters shall* ***prophesy****, your old men shall* ***dream dreams****, your young men shall* ***see visions".***

Do you not find it interesting that in this famous passage here about the outpouring of the Holy Spirit, the things God promised would accompany receiving the Holy Spirit? *Prophesying, seeing visions, dreaming dreams.* Where is the mention of the performing of miracles and the healing of the sick? No mention of them here. Would you not have expected Him to have highlighted first and foremost these more dynamic gifts? After all, these are the gifts, which capture people's attention more than anything else. These are generally the gifts that attract people from all walks of life and motivate them to fill auditoriums all over our cities, so they can hear and see the evangelists who possess these gifts. But no, the ones He highlights here are these comparatively unimpressive and seemingly passive gifts.

Had it been us, no doubt, we would have done the very opposite. These power gifts are the very ones we would first be highlighting one would receive after receiving the Holy Spirit. Possibly, they would be on our campaign posters and our advertising billboards. Of course, we know that all of these gifts or power ministries are some things that receiving the baptism of the Holy Spirit brings with it, but God here in this prophecy does not mention them. Instead, He mentions *prophesying, dreaming dreams and seeing visions*.

Now, did God omit to mention these other power gifts because He feels they are not important? Of course not. We only have to read through the Book of Acts and first Corinthians to see that this is not the case. I believe He mentions instead, having visions and dreams because He wants us to understand the amazing life-changing power that lies in having visions and dreams that are given by the Holy Spirit. In the aforementioned scripture, we are going to be looking at what I believe are a number of very important principles. These are essential principles for us to be aware of if we are going to understand the power of having visions and dreams, and also to have success in those visions and dreams.

Here Are Six Principles to Guide Us Towards Making Our Dreams and Visions Possible

- *Your vision is given to you for those whom you are meant to inspire*
- *Your vision must be written down*
- *Your vision must be clear*
- *Your vision must be written in the hearts of people*
- *Your vision is for a specific time*
- *Clear written visions will always escalate progress*

Throughout this book, we are going to look at these six principles and see how they relate to us in establishing and fulfilling our vision and dreams.

"Every vision has in it all the resources to service that vision."

Unknown

CHAPTER 4

FIRST PRINCIPLE

"Your vision is given to you for those whom you are meant to inspire"

In this chapter, we will be looking at our verse of focus in Habakkuk and breaking it down. In doing so, I want to highlight what I believe are principles that govern having a vision. The very first thing to know about your visions and dreams is that **your vision was not given to you for your sake alone. The truth is, it was given to you for those whom you are meant to inspire and help to fulfil their God-given purpose in life**. This I believe is principle number one. As the passage states, *"that they may run that read it." Habakkuk 2:2 (KJV)* If that is so, then having dreams and visions carries with it tremendous responsibilities. A responsibility to God first of all who gives those visions and dreams. We must take the responsibility and the care to ensure that we both capture and convey the vision exactly as God gave it to us. Then secondly, to the people for whom those visions were given, that when they read it, it clearly directs them to God's purpose for their lives.

Take, for example, the reason God stated in His Word for calling and commissioning Joshua to be a leader to His people. What He said to Joshua, I believe is the purpose why God gives a vision to anyone. *"Be strong and of a good courage:* ***for unto this people shalt thou divide for an inheritance the land, which I swore unto their fathers to give them"***. Joshua 1:6 *(KJV)* **So there you see it. He was called and commissioned to help others to inherit what God had promised them.**

This is an awesome scripture. It gives us a beautiful picture of what being given a vision is all about. His calling, his gifting, his anointing, and his charge to Joshua were to help others to inherit what God had promised them. It was not for himself; it was for others. Do you know that Joshua did not receive his own inheritance until the very end when he had fulfilled his charge to divide the land among the twelve tribes? How amazing!

It is the same for us today. Our giftings, our anointing, our ministry, our abilities, whatever they might be, are all given to us for the benefit of others. Sadly, so many people mistake their gifting as God's reward to them for good behaviour or as a repayment for their length of faithful service. No, your vision was not given to you for yourself, but primarily for others' benefit. I believe that there are many people in our world today who are walking around poor, impoverished, and unsuccessful, all because the key persons who could have inspired and motivated them to be successful are living their lives without a vision or dream. Think about that.

I often think about the very famous and iconic speech delivered by the late Dr Martin Luther King Jr and the historical impact it has made, even on our present generation. His dream made him look forward to a day when a man would be judged, not by the colour of his skin but by the content of his character. The amazing thing for me about that vision is that it was held by someone who was rejected by the very society that he was having the vision for. Also, it was said in a time when the majority of that society did not welcome or embrace that vision. On the face of it, it seemed completely impossible that such a thing could ever become a reality. Yet just a generation later, we saw a leader, a person of colour, against all the odds, being elected to the highest office, not only in that nation but in the entire world.

On the 20th of January 2008, President Barak Obama was inaugurated as the President of the United States of America. He was the first African American to have done so in the very history of that nation. This fulfils the audacious vision of Dr Martin Luther King Jr.; something that many thought was impossible to happen. That's the amazing power there is in having visions and dreams. Like small seeds that are sown, it is hard to imagine that the lofty trees that they produce actually came from those seeds. All things, Jesus said are possible to him who believes.

The fact is, this troubled world of ours is littered with such inspiring cases where against all the odds, some unlikely person emerges with a dream so audacious and ridiculous that some would even question the state of mind of the dreamer. Only to see just a little further down the road, seemingly mysterious forces set in motion some series of events that end up bringing that very vision to pass. I think of Gandhi, that petite, harmless-looking, self-effacing figure, who through his peaceful protest, took on the might of the powerful British Empire and gained self-rule for his country. Convicted and inspired by his vision, he and his followers challenged the status quo and refused to give up their dream; and in the end, his dreams became a reality. It is said that it is not the size of the man that has the dream, but the size of the dream that is in the man.

I am afraid there are no shortcuts to this. It is a law. Life yields its fruits to those who make a demand upon it. Speaking of the Kingdom of God, Jesus Himself states in the gospel of Matthew, 11:12. *"From the days of John the Baptist, the Kingdom of God suffers violence and the violent take it by force."* I love how the Amplified Version of the Bible puts it. *"From the days of John the Baptist until now, the kingdom of heaven* ***suffers violent assault, and violent men seize it by force as a precious prize****."*

What Jesus is clearly saying here is that His Kingdom does not come to those who sit around waiting for when it suits God to bring it to them. No, it comes to those who **clearly see the vision of the Kingdom as a prize, a pearl of great price and puts every effort and everything he possesses into gaining it.** All things are possible to him who believes.

Even God Himself wrote down His vision for His people when He gave them the law.

CHAPTER 5

SECOND PRINCIPLE

"Your vision must be written down"

Then we come to the other very famous passage in the scriptures that speaks about the power of vision. *"Write the* ***vision*** *and* ***make it plain UPON TABLES.*** *Habakkuk 2:2* (KJV)

Wow! There is so much in that one sentence, but we will deal with the second part later. Firstly, it tells us that the vision **has to be written.** Yes, I believe that a vision must be written. This is the first step in establishing a vision. "Oh, that is pretty obvious," you say. However, you would be surprised just how many people do not actually write down their visions or dreams. It is in their head only. "Why write it down if I know where I'm going?" Some folks may ask, only to find further on down the road that life, age, and time have conspired against them, and their visions and dreams have dissipated like the morning mist.

Even God Himself wrote down His vision for how He wanted His people to live when He gave them the law. The Ten Commandments were God's vision of how He wanted His covenant people to live and so He wanted to make it crystal clear to them so He wrote it Himself. In Exodus 31:18, the scripture tells us, *"When He (God) had finished speaking with him (Moses) on Mount Sinai, He gave Moses the two tablets of the testimony, tables of Stone,* ***written with the finger of God." AMP.*** Even the very kings of Israel were commanded to write out a personal copy of the law for themselves to guide them in their rule, despite the fact that the nation itself already had one. *"And when he sits on the throne of his kingdom,* ***he shall write for himself in a book a copy of this law approved by the Levitical priests."*** *Deuteronomy 17:18 (KJV)*

So yes, your vision should be written. And so, as long as your vision is in your head only, it is abstract; it is unclear; and therefore, it cannot possibly be clear to others. Furthermore, considering that our vision primarily benefits others, we have a huge responsibility to write it down.

"Can the blind lead the blind, shall they not both fall into the ditch"?

- *Luke 6:39 (KJV)*

CHAPTER 6

THIRD PRINCIPLE

"Your vision must be clear"

Then, in writing it, the Bible says, ***you have to make it plain (or make it easy to be understood)***. The actual word in Hebrew for *plain* is the word *Ba'ar;* and it comes from a root word which means, ***to dig, to explain or to engrave.*** This is crucial. The implication of this statement is that you have to put so much effort into making your vision clear that it is as though you have dug and engraved it. The wise man Solomon states: *"A word fitly spoken is like apples of gold in* ***pictures*** *of silver."* Proverbs 25:11 (KJV) The word picture there in Hebrew speaks of *"a figure carved on stone."* So then, this suggest that to make your vision plain and clear, speaks of intentionality, purposefulness, and effort. So, as it is said, *"let us choose our words wisely for they are the architect of reality."* How many people put any effort of that kind into their vision? But according to the scripture, for it to be successful, you must.

Now, the explanation is clear, but the question is, where is this engraving to be done? We will look at this point later.

Here are Some questions to think about:

What about your marriage? How important is it that both you and your partner are clear about where you are going in your marriage? Do you both have a vision or dream for your marriage or are you just drifting by from year to year? And what about your family? How important is it to you that your children see and understand clearly where you are trying to get to as a family? I would say that this is essential if you really are serious about achieving anything as a family. Then what about you Pastors? Do you have any visions or dreams for your church or your ministry? Are you clear about what God wants you to do? Is it clear to those who are following you where you are going or when you plan to get there? Here is another point that folks rarely discover if they are not serious about their goals. What exactly is going to be the cost of achieving your vision? The harsh fact is that every vision, however small, has a cost factor. That is one of the main considerations that must be factored into your vision.

"Forasmuch as ye are manifestly declared to be the epistle of Christ ***ministered by us, written not with ink, but with the Spirit of the living God; not in tables of stone, but in fleshy tables of the heart."***

- 2 Corinthians 3:3 (KJV)

CHAPTER 7

WRITING THE VISION

On a personal level, I well remember when I first got married to my first wife, who has now passed away. When we started our family, we wanted our children to have a particular mindset towards learning from a very young age. Of course, the first goal we tried to establish in their lives was for them to give their lives to the Lord Jesus and to live for Him. We then wanted them to start having dreams and visions for their lives, even before they properly understood anything about what visions and dreams were.

Having an understanding of the extreme importance of someone's mindset in his or her ultimate success, we wanted them from that very young age to begin to try to cultivate a visionary mindset, to practise dreaming – and also to dream big. We wanted it to become as natural to them as learning any subject whilst they were still in primary education. To help in their academic achievement, my wife and I used to say to them things like: "when you become a doctor," "when you become an architect," or "when you become a lawyer" as though this was a foregone conclusion that this was the path they were going to take in life.

Yes, of course, they walked around telling their friends and teachers that they were going to be doctors, and architects and lawyers and so on when they grew up. And yes, I know we could not predict what their futures were going to be, because, at the end of the day, we knew that this ultimately was dependent on God's will for their lives, coupled with their choices. And no, they did not become architects, doctors, or lawyers, but they all succeeded in equally responsible professions.

In fact, our youngest daughter is a teacher; she has had her first book published and is now a pastor's wife. The oldest girl is a dietician. She is also in joint leadership ministry with her husband in her church. Then the youngest boy is a very successful computer graphic artist who has his own company. He has worked in designing some of the most successful products in the world. In fact, he is the one who designed the cover for this book. However, most successful of all, they are all serving the Lord Jesus Christ. Well, am I saying that training them to think in this certain way was what caused them to be where they are? I am saying that our mindset, visions and dreams for our lives all put us on a certain trajectory that can help us to discover God's ultimate plans and purpose for our lives. The important thing to me in all of this is the mindset we adopt as our *modus operandi* in life. As the wise man Solomon said, *"as a man thinks in his heart, so is he."* (Proverbs 23:7 NKJV) *So* in effect, we are no greater or lesser than our thoughts.

So, let me ask again, what about within your own life? Your business? Your marriage? What progress do you think you can make if there is ambiguity about the vision you have for your future? If you are not clear about where you are going, your destination will also remain ambiguous upon your arrival.

"Keep thy heart with all diligence for out of it are the issues of life."

- *Proverbs 4:23 (KJV)*

CHAPTER 8

FOURTH PRINCIPLE

"Your vision must be written in the heart"

Then the fourth principle; and in my opinion, probably the most important of all and it is about where this vision or dream is to be written or engraved. This is critical. The scripture says, ***they are to be written on TABLES.***

In the olden days, people did not have books like we have today. They wrote things on parchments or tablets made of clay. Of course, God does not expect us in this computer age to still be writing things on clay tablets or on parchments. We can still do so if we so desire, but those tablets and parchments were only a type of what God intended in the church age. God's Word states that *the vision has to be written on tables or engraved on tables.* Therefore, the question is, which table is it that God is speaking about? Our dining tables? Or our dressing tables? Definitely, not!

In 2 Corinthians 3:3 (KJV), Paul clarifies for us what these tablets or tables are.

> *"Forasmuch as ye are manifestly declared to be the epistle of Christ* ***ministered by us, written not with ink, but with the Spirit of the living God; not in tables of stone, but in fleshy tables of the heart."***

There it is. Not on earthly tablets or parchments anymore; not even on our computers or laptops, but on the very hearts of people. **Yes, God's vision must be made plain, written and engraved on our hearts if we are ever going to be successful.**

How very sad that there are so many of God's wonderful people in the pews of our churches who have no vision whatsoever to follow. You have good, sincere, hard-working pastors, also with very active and enthusiastic church members but without a clear vision. Very sadly and very often, they see little fruit for their hard work. These members are just going with the flow and enjoying the ride, but they have no idea where they are riding or flowing to. It is a fact that if you do not know where you are going, you may get there, but when you do have an idea where you are going, there is no stopping you.

Then we see some couples and families working hard to be successful, but sadly, they too see little progress in their work because they lack a clear vision of their goals. None for their marriages, none for their families, none for their careers and none for their financial success. Sadly, they will have little or no success to celebrate in the future if nothing changes. Therefore, without a vision, the people perish, as revealed in *Proverbs 29:18 (KJV). This could be interpreted as people just living their lives without self-control and without any serious care for their future.*

"To everything there is a season and a time to every purpose under the heaven."

Ecclesiastes 3:1(KJV)

CHAPTER 9

FIFTH PRINCIPLE

"Your vision is for a specific time"

And so, God told the prophet Habakkuk to write the vision on tablets. This was for a number of reasons. Firstly, ***because the vision was for an appointed time.*** **Yes, there is always an appointed time for your vision.** The wise man Solomon said, *"To everything, there is a season and a time to every purpose under the sun." Ecclesiastes 3:1 KJV.* Visions are not for the present; they are always for the future. Just like seeds that we plant, they never produce in the seasons that we plant them. The fruits always come in a totally different season. Therefore, it needs real patience if you will see your vision come to pass.

Listen to what the Lord said to Habakkuk. *"For the vision is* ***yet for the appointed [future] time.*** *It hurries toward the goal [of fulfilment]; it will not fail. Even though it delays, wait* *[patiently] for it, because it will certainly come; it will not delay"*. Habakkuk 2:3 (AMP)

So many people have visions today and expect it to come to pass tomorrow. As we have established before, it takes time; and the thing is, God Himself is the One who sets the time for the fulfilment of your vision. How often is it repeated in Scripture and *"when the time of the promise drew near"* God acted?

I remember growing up as a boy in Jamaica, about five or six years of age. I used to follow my father around, completely fascinated as he tended his garden. He seemed to possess a gift to produce the most delicious vegetables in the smallest patch of ground. Sometimes, he would give me a seed or a young plant for me to plant for myself. However, I was so impatient that every day I would go and dig up that seed to see if it was growing. I guess you can imagine what happened to that poor little plant. I was not patient enough to wait for the right season.

Well, every vision is a seed. As we all know, seeds need time to grow. Therefore, when the time comes for whom, the vision was given, likewise, the Word of the Lord will come to the one who needs it so *that he may run who reads it* in the right season. So, let me say it again, every seed that is planted, whether physical or spiritual has to wait for a totally different season to see fruit from that seed.

Joseph was seventeen years old when God began to give him some amazing visions for his life. He then went through some of the worst experiences that made it seem as though his dreams would never come to pass. It was not until some thirteen years later, after he had gone through trial after trial that Joseph began to see and experience some of what God told him would come to pass. Can you imagine the mental and emotional conflict he must have gone through as his life went from one crisis to another? Struggling to make sense of what was happening to him; struggling to keep his integrity and maintain his faith in God.

On the face of it, it could even seem as though God Himself was against him rather than with him. It is as though the searing heat of tribulation was going to make his vision wither. However, just as the heat of the sun makes a plant grow, likewise, trials and tribulations are always the climate that makes a vision that is really written in the heart bear fruit…and so Joseph held on.

As with all seeds that are sown, the seasons change, and harvest time comes around. The Bible said, that as long as the earth remains, *"there will always be seed time and harvest," Genesis 8:22 (KJV).* Even so, with the seeds of our vision and dreams, harvest time will come around - and so it did for Joseph. The Bible said, *"They bruised his feet with shackles and placed his neck in irons, until his (God's) prediction came true and the word of the LORD proved him right.* ***The king sent and released him; the ruler of peoples set him free.****"* *Psalm 105:19-2 (BSB)* *This* was the beginning of a brand-new season for Joseph.

Then what about Abraham, the father of our faith? He waited even longer; twenty-five long years before he saw the first blade of God's vision for his life begin to sprout. Yes, God promised him that he was going to have children as innumerable as the stars of heaven and as the sand of the seashore. But waiting twenty-five years for something that God promised you, something that you have no power whatsoever to bring about by your efforts, can be extremely discouraging. I am sure that this was maybe how Abraham and Sarah felt sometimes; and as a result, he got distracted. His distraction led him to go and father a child with his wife's maid, Hagar. And the reason why he got distracted? The season for the vision had not yet arrived.

But God kept pointing him back to His promises and His purpose for His life and, as we know, in the right time, in harvest time, it finally came to pass. We can therefore take heart in holding on to our vision because God is always true to His Word.

So, there it is, where there is a clear written vision, there can be progress. This progress though, is only for those to whom it is clear enough to be able to read it. That is the positive power of visions or dreams. It will empower you to run the race successfully and speedily, but also patiently. So many capable lives with amazing potential could have gone much further and soared much higher, impacted greater, had they had a clear vision or dream written in their hearts.

HOW IS THE VISION WRITTEN?

Now the question is, if the ultimate place that a vision is to be written is on the hearts of people, how then is that vision to be written? Paul again states it in 2 Corinthians 3:3 (NKJV)

> *"You are our epistle written in our hearts, known and read by all men; clearly you* ***are an epistle of Christ,*** *MINISTERED BY US,* ***written not with ink but by the Spirit of the living God, not on tablets of stone but on tablets of flesh, that is, of the heart."***

Yes, by the preaching and the teaching of God's powerful Word, the revelation of God's truth is written on the tables of our hearts. The Apostle John states the same thing in his third epistle; 3 John 13-14 (NIV). *"**I have much to write you,** but **I do not want to do so with pen and ink**. I hope to see you soon, and we will talk face to face."*

John was going to wait until he saw the church face to face to write what he wanted to say *on* the hearts of his hearers. Until your visions and dreams are made so plain in your hearts that it feels like it has been engraved, then it is doubtful whether there will be success in your vision.

He sends forth Him commandment upon the earth: His word runs very swiftly."

- *Psalms 147:15 (NKJV)*

CHAPTER 10

SIXTH PRINCIPLE

"Your vision will escalate Progress"

THE ESCALATION OF THE VISION

Then we come to the sixth and final principle. Habakkuk 2:2b (BSB) *"So that he may RUN (not walk) who reads it"*. Isn't that inspiring? This is one of the most positive aspects of having a clear vision. **It will escalate and greatly speed up your progress.**

Now tell me, who does not want this kind of speedy progress for their lives or their ministry? Or who does not want to see the speedy success of those who follow their vision? We all want to make a speedy success of our lives and ministries. Well, at least I do! I have never once heard someone express frustration or complain that their dreams have come to pass too quickly. Have you? However, I have heard numberless complaints from all kinds of people about how long their dreams have taken to come to pass. We all want to have speedy success.

But according to the above-mentioned scripture, this escalation of the fulfilment of our dreams and visions can only be achieved when they are made plain and written on tables.

There is an extremely interesting scripture in Exodus 34:29-35 (KJV), which relates well to our subject here.

> *When Moses came down from Mount Sinai with the two tablets of the covenant law in his hands, he was not aware that his face was radiant because he had spoken with the Lord. When Aaron and all the Israelites saw Moses, his face was radiant, and they were afraid to come near him. But Moses called to them; so Aaron and all the leaders of the community came back to him, and he spoke to them. Afterward all the Israelites came near him, and he gave them all the commands the Lord had given him on Mount Sinai. When Moses finished speaking to them,* ***he put a veil over his face****. But whenever he entered the Lord's presence to speak with him, he removed the veil until he came out. And when he came out and told the Israelites what he had been commanded, they saw that his face was radiant.* ***Then***

Moses would put the veil back over his face until he went in to speak with the Lord.

The Apostle Paul refers to this passage in 2 Corinthians 3:13 (NIV). "Therefore, since we have such a hope, we are very bold. ***We are not like Moses who put a veil over his face to keep the Israelites from gazing the end of what was fading away. But their minds were closed. For to this day, the same veil remains at the reading of the Old Covenant. It has not been lifted, because only in Christ can it be removed."*** What an awesome scripture!

Somehow, this good-intentioned act of Moses, of putting a veil over his face to accommodate the close fellowship of the children of Israel after coming back from the presence of the Lord, actually damaged the progress of both those poor fearful Israelites and their entire generations after them. **That veil, rather than becoming a help to the nation, became a hindrance. In some mysterious way, that act became symbolic and cast a spiritual shadow over the nation in their understanding of the Old Testament. It did not speed up their progress, it slowed down or stopped the entire nation from seeing God's plan and purpose clearly.**

Paul purposed as a result, that in this case, he did not want to be like Moses. How could he avoid becoming like Moses? He tells us in 2 Corinthians 3:12 (NIV);

"Seeing then that we have such hope, we use ***great plainness of speech****."* In other words, he does not want to obscure the vision by using words or preaching that does not make the vision of God's purpose as plain as can be. This is the tremendous responsibility that this generation of Christians has in sharing the gospel to this present lost generation. We have to make the gospel so plain that even a blind person will be able to see it clearly.

"The greatest people in the world are dreamers. They invent things before they are created."

- Emile Austin

CHAPTER 11

VISIONARIES ARE WORLD CHANGERS

Visionaries are world changers. They are always the ones who make a difference in this world. Visionaries and dreamers have made every single and significant change that has taken place in the world. They are always the ones who change the status quo. I am sure you have heard about Thomas Edison (1847-1931), one of the world's greatest inventors and scientists. He is credited with developing the light bulb. After evidently attempting some thousands of times to invent this light bulb, reporters asked him; "Dr Eddison, why do you not give up having failed so many times? His reply was, "At least I know thousands of ways in which it will not work." How amazing! Can we relate to such tenacity today? As a result of this man's belief in his vision, billions of people all over this entire planet are benefitting from his vision.

Then there are the Wright Brothers (1867-1912). They were credited with making the very first aircraft flight.

These brothers dreamed of a machine that would fly in the air. Can you imagine the amount of ridicule they must have experienced by those who did not share their vision? In fact, it is said that they were ridiculed as *"cranks and fools"* for having such dreams. In their first successful attempt, that first aircraft flew for just twelve seconds and covered one hundred and twenty feet. To the world then, this was a historic event. Twelve seconds and one hundred and twenty feet. Not very earth-shattering, you might say. Now, the fastest man-made craft we have to date is the Parker Solar Probe which evidently travels at an amazing four hundred thousand miles per hour. Yes, you did read that correctly. This is a staggering one hundred and ten miles per second.

When you look at it, that first solo flight was not so much for those brothers or even that generation, but it was primarily for us who have seemingly perfected that first attempt. To this day, I sometimes think about these two brothers whenever I hop on a flight to go somewhere. From that seed of a vision to where we are today. The vision is always for an appointed time.

Still, another invention that is absolutely relevant to our generation is the telephone. This invention was credited to Alexander Graham Bell (1847 – 1922). Even as the visionary that he was, I am certain he could never have imagined just how very different the world would be today because of that first step in his invention.

Another great visionary was Booker T. Washington (1856 – 1915). He was born into slavery in a nation that legalised this inhumane practice. His mother was a cook for a plantation owner, and his father was a white slave owner whom he never knew. At the close of the American Civil War, all the slaves owned by their owners, James and Elizabeth Burroughs, were freed. This included Booker T Washington's mother and his siblings. He was only allowed to attend school after working from 4 a.m. to 9 a.m. each day in a local salt-works. In a second job in a local coal mine, he overheard two workers speaking about the Hampton Institute, a school for ex-slaves in West Virginia. This ignited a spark in the heart of Booker T Washington.

So strong was his dream that in 1872, Booker T. Washington walked 500 miles to Hampton to attend the school. He was an excellent student, as you can imagine. Because of his strong dreams, amongst all his other achievements, he became an American educator, author, orator, and advisor to several presidents of the United States.

It is not always where you begin that determines where you end up. The most beautiful plants are grown in dirt.

Some of the world's most amazing and expensive works of art were painted in grubby and dirty studios. *"Even the very spider takes hold with his hands and is found in the king's palaces,"* the wise man Solomon says in Proverbs 30:28 (NKJV). Yes, dreamers are world changers. It is through their visions that they have changed the direction of mankind.

Do you know that today, most successful companies employ people to just dream, to innovate and generate new ideas? They know if they are ever going to stay one step ahead of their competitors and be successful in the marketplace, they must constantly come up with new ideas. They reinvest a large percentage of their profit into the company just for this purpose.

God also uses visionaries and dreamers to bring changes in His Kingdom. They are the vehicles who God uses to bring about His plans for the world. They are the vessels through whom He pours the healing ointment of His Spirit to the growing needs of mankind. It is no surprise to me, then that having visions and dreams are some of the major gifts the Holy Spirit comes to give us through the powerful baptism of the Holy Spirit. Seeing the power of visions, no longer makes me think of these gifts as passive. They are invested with limitless possibilities, power and wealth.

Someone once said some of the wealthiest places in the world are not the gold or diamond mines of Africa or the oil fields of the various parts of the world. Rather, the wealthiest places on the planet are just down the road from each of us. You will find them in every community in every country. It is the cemetery. There lie buried limitless treasures of inventions that were never made, bestselling books that were never written, masterpieces that were never painted, mega-structures that were never built, companies that were never started and of course, powerful anointed ministries that could have transformed multitudes in this broken world of ours. Yes, in our cemeteries lies buried the greatest treasure of unrealised potential, unfulfilled dreams and aborted visions.

Although this is largely true, I would, however, like to make one modification to that statement and it is this. It is not the cemetery which is the wealthiest place on this planet. No. It is the hearts and lives that carry the God-given visions and dreams that God has entrusted to us that are still being realised. Who can quantify what untold wealth, prosperity and blessings are being carried around in the many visions God has given different people among us? I am absolutely convinced that we have still not yet seen the full potential that lies in the hearts of people to whom God has given visions;

visions that are meant to be a blessing to the world. Let us remember those astounding words God said of the generation in the Book of Genesis. *"Now, nothing shall be restrained (impossible) from them which they have imagined to do."* Could the visions and dreams that God has given you be one of those that will change this sin-sick world today?

"And it shall come to pass afterward that I will pour out My Spirit upon all flesh; and your sons and your daughters shall prophesy, your old men shall dream dreams, your young men shall see visions;"

- Joel 2: 28 (KJV)

CHAPTER 12

WHO THEN SHOULD DREAM OR HAVE A VISION?

Who then should dream dreams and have visions? Should it just be the pastors, the preachers and the company directors? God has created every single one of us with the capacity to dream and have visions. The only people who can be excused from having dreams are those who are dead!

Even in nature, not being able to dream is abnormal. I read somewhere that scientists had discovered that if people do not dream at night, they become unhealthy. Isn't that telling?

- ✓ Therefore, every mother who gives birth should have dreams for their children.
- ✓ Every man who has ever fathered a child should have dreams and visions for that child.
- ✓ No parent should wait until the child grows up before they start dreaming for that child. In fact,

before they begin to have children, they should already be dreamers.

- ✓ Every boy and every girl growing up as soon as they can be taught to dream, should begin to have dreams for their lives.
- ✓ Married couples should have lots of dreams for their lives.
- ✓ The middle-aged people, the old men and women should have dreams. (Joseph had dreams of his people leaving Egypt.)
- ✓ The poor especially should have dreams.
- ✓ The down and out should have dreams. Those who have failed in education or business should have dreams.
- ✓ Now here is an interesting one. Those who are successful should also have visions and dreams. They need to dream about how best to manage their success.
- ✓ The Christian, the Sunday School Teacher, the Youth Leader, the Deacons, the Deaconesses, the Ushers; not to mention of course, Preachers and Pastors, should be the greatest dreamers of all.
- ✓ Lastly, leaders of nations, prime ministers, and presidents should have dreams. It is tragic to see many nations with vast resources of wealth enough to bless not only their own nation, but the

entire world suffering in abject poverty, all because their leaders or governments have no vision or dream.

WHAT SHOULD BE THE DIMENSION OF MY DREAM?

We now come to a point we mentioned at the very beginning of this book. Some folks have small dreams, not because they are not capable, but because they suffer from an inferiority complex. They feel that there is an incongruity between them and their dreams. So let me ask. What should be the dimension or the size of your dreams or your vision? How big should my dream be?

Personally, I believe that our dreams should be as huge as possible, simply because I believe God wants to give us big dreams. I came across a scripture years ago which changed my perspective of God forever. See if you can digest it. This is speaking about Abraham.

> *"For the promise, that he should be the HEIR OF THE WORLD was not to Abraham, or to his seed, through the law, but through the righteousness of faith"* Romans 4:13 (KJV).

Has it hit you? God made Abraham the heir of the world. Can we conceive a greater vision than this? Then God led Abram outside and said,

- *"Look at the sky. There are so many stars you cannot count them. Your descendants also will be too many to count."* And he brought him forth abroad, and said,
- *"look now toward heaven, and number the stars, if thou be able to number them: and he said unto him, so shall thy seed be."*

Again, God told him; *"In your seed shall all the nations of the world be blessed."* Genesis 22:18 (KJV) The heir of the world. In your seed shall all the nations of the world be blessed. This is the vision that God gave a human being; a man whose wife was past child-bearing age and a man whose body was heading in the same way. And you know the amazing thing? God is still bringing this promise to pass every single day that this world is going on.

What about little "daddy's boy' Joseph? Before God spoke to Him, could we see him any different from running errands for Jacob? However, God's vision for this little shepherd boy was that he would become the prime minister of the greatest empire on the earth at that time. Who in the world could have seen that coming?

Only a God who has great delight in giving us visions that are way beyond what we are even able to conceive for our lives. *He is able to do exceeding, abundantly, above ALL that we are able to ask or even think. Ephesians 3:20* (KJV)

But whether our dreams are supernaturally given to us by God, or we dream them as goals for our lives, I believe we should dream as big as we possibly can; bigger than what we can naturally achieve by ourselves. As having visions and dreams is one of the results of the outpouring of the Holy Ghost, I firmly believe that God will give the level of anointing it requires to fulfil the dreams He has given to every life, whatever its size.

"And Joseph dreamed a dream and told it to his brethren and they hated him yet the more."

- Genesis 37:5 (KJV)

CHAPTER 13

COST OF YOUR DREAM

We come now to the part of having a vision or a dream that we sometimes do not like to face, and that is the cost. Yes, there is a cost to you having a vision or a dream. There is always a cost. Being called by God to share His message of love and repentance with the world that is hostile to Him is costly. Often, this can demand more from you than you feel you possess, or that you feel capable of giving. Your dream may take you completely out of your comfort zone; out of your feeling of sufficiency; and may even make you become the most unpopular. Jesus says, "No man lights a candle and puts it under a bushel." No, he changes that candle's position once it is lit, and puts it in the most prominent place so that all can benefit from the light. Now to those of us who are shy and introverted by nature and do not like the limelight, but prefer working in the background, this may be very difficult, being placed on a candlestick for all to see. This was a huge problem for me; and even after all these years in ministry, in some instances, I still find it to be a challenge. It may require you to develop skills that you had not planned on learning. For others, it may be to reach out to cultures that you are not used to; but whatever it is, there will always be a cost.

Take the prophets of old and the apostles in the early church, called in many cases to give messages to people who sometimes did not want to hear them. Many have even lost their very lives in doing so. Jesus clearly warned them whilst He was with them that this would be a possibility. *"Some of you they will kill and think they are doing God's service."* And true to His Word, practically every single one of those apostles was persecuted or killed because they shared the vision of the gospel. Sadly, in different parts of the world, Christians today are still paying this ultimate cost of sharing the vision of the gospel.

However, it is not all negative. Let's look again at the inspiring example of Joseph. Just a teenager, seventeen years of age when God interrupted his young life and began to give him His vision for his life. God's vision for Joseph came to him in the comfort of his special loving relationship with his father and in the comfort of his home and country. This vision, however, was not meant to be fulfilled in the comfort zone of the special relationship with his father or his home or nation. No, the vision was to find its fulfilment in Egypt, some seven hundred miles away.

The amazing thing is, no one would have guessed that this was where his dream was going to be fulfilled. There was no reason for him to go to Egypt. Jacob had no family there, neither was he doing any business that required him to go to Egypt and take his household with him. God, however, always has His way of bringing to pass what He has promised.

Well, as most dreamers do, they assume that those around them will be excited for them that God actually wants to use their life. Unfortunately, this is not always so. Already hated by his brothers because of their father's partiality towards him, it was not difficult for the brothers' hatred and rejection of Joseph to escalate, especially now that he was also having dreams.

> *"And Joseph dreamed a dream and told it to his brethren and they hated him yet the more." Genesis 37:5 (KJV).*

There is a cost to every dream. The situation got even worse when the brothers heard the content of the dream, for it had implications that none of them could stomach.

> *"We were binding sheaves of grain in the field, and suddenly my sheaf rose and stood upright, while your*

> *sheaves gathered around and bowed down to mine."* Genesis 37:7 (KJV)

Without exception, they all saw the clear implication of the dream and voiced their consternation.

> *"And his brothers said to him, "Shall you indeed reign over us? Or shall you indeed have dominion over us?" So they hated him even more for his dreams and for his words." Genesis 37:8 (KJV)*

Unfortunately, his problems did not stop there. If anything, they got even worse. Why? He had another dream.

> *9 Then Joseph had another dream and told it to his brothers. "Look," he said, "I had another dream, and this time the sun and moon and eleven stars were bowing down to me." 10 He told his father and brothers, but his father rebuked him and said, "What is this dream that you have had? Will your mother and brothers and I actually come and bow down to the ground before you?"* Genesis 37:9-10 (KJV)

This time he told not just his brothers, but also his father. No doubt he expected his father to understand and support him. Rather than understanding, the Bible says, *"his father rebuked him"*. How much worse could it get? As I have said before, there is a cost to every dream. Not everyone will believe in your dreams; understand your dreams; or even love you for your dreams. Just remember this: dreams are God's plan for your future.

Now the question is, how is God going to get Joseph to the place where his dreams will be fulfilled? As I have said before, God always has a plan for the fulfilment of His vision. Sent by his father to check up on his brothers, who were meant to be looking after their father's sheep, Joseph went looking for them. Spotting them afar off, his very own brothers began to plot against him.

> *"But they saw him in the distance, and before he reached them, they plotted to kill him. "Here comes that dreamer!" they said to each other. "Come now, let's kill him and throw him into one of these cisterns and say that a ferocious animal devoured him. Then we'll see what comes of his dreams."* Genesis 37: 18-20 (NKJV)

How incredible that someone's dreams can evoke such hostility and hatred, especially from those whom you would expect to love you the most? Isn't this the very same thing the leaders of Israel did to Jesus? He came with the vision of building His Father's Kingdom, but the leaders were threatened by His vision. And as the Lord highlighted in the parable, He taught in Mark 12:1-

11 (KJV); specifically, in verse 7 they said; *"This is the heir, let us kill Him and the inheritance shall be ours."*

And so young Joseph was plucked from the love of his father, from his home and his country. The brothers in their hatred kidnapped him, threw him in a pit, and then sold him for the price of a slave to Midianites. These Midianites took him to Egypt and then sold him to Potiphar, who was one of Pharaoh's ministers. As incredible and horrible as this was, this was the path that led Joseph to the very place where the fulfilment of his dream would eventually take place. His path was the cost he had to pay. The amazing wisdom and power of our God!

As I have said before, there is always a cost for your dreams. So, the question is, are you prepared to pay the cost of having a vision? Are you prepared to live within the restricted lifestyle a vision imposes on you? It does not allow you to cast off restraint and to live any old how as those without a vision do. It is living a life spent serving others; your life is no longer your own. But as the Lord says, and as visionaries and dreamers discover, it is in losing our lives living in this way that we really find it, when our lives are lived for Him.

The end of this story is one that always leaves me speechless even after reading this account countless times throughout the years. And why is this? Simply because Joseph would eventually be the saviour of those very brothers who hated him, and of the father who rebuked him for those very same visions and dreams. There is always a cost for your vision; and the thing is, people need to see first of all the price you are willing to pay to see those dreams come to pass before they are willing to follow you or believe in you.

"It is said, "the greatest oak comes from a little nut who held its ground."

- *Author unknown.*

CHAPTER 14

LEARNING TO BE VISIONARY

Now, the million-dollar question is, how do we become dreamers? How do we develop our visions and dreams? Is being visionary something that can be developed and learned? Without any shadow of a doubt, yes!

For me, training ourselves to be a visionary and thinking big begins with **first accepting the vision of the gospel or God's very own vision for His church.** It is amazing to think that even God has visions and dreams. This is the starting point. We as Christians must be convinced, committed, and consumed by the vision of the gospel. This wonderful gospel is a part of God's very own vision for His church. Not only that, but it is in the gospel where all of us, as the church of Jesus Christ, find our corporate and individual purpose. In the Book of Corinthians, the Bible states; "*And God has placed in the church first of all apostles, second prophets, third teachers, then miracles, then gifts of healing, of helping, of guidance, and of different kinds of tongues.*" 1Corinthians 12:28 (KJV)

Then, in the Book of Romans, we see Paul giving another list of gifts that God has also placed in the church. "*So in Christ we who are many are one body, and each member belongs to one another.* ***We have different gifts according to the grace given us. If one's gift is prophecy, let him use it in proportion to his faith;*** *if it is serving, let him serve; if it is teaching, let him teach.*" Romans 12:5-6 (BSB)

So, amongst all of these dynamic power gifts and the not-so-dynamic ordinary and everyday gifts, such as helping or serving, or even being an encourager, we all have a place in there somewhere. So let us begin by accepting God's vision for His church. It is the greatest vision there is. God's plan for His church in a nutshell, I believe, can be summarised as this:

- LOVE GOD WITH ALL OUR HEARTS, SOUL MIND AND STRENGTH.
- GO INTO ALL THE WORLD AND PREACH THE GOSPEL TO EVERY SINGLE CREATURE.
- ONE DAY JESUS IS COMING BACK TO TAKE US TO LIVE WITH HIM FOREVER.
- HE WILL REWARD US WAY BEYOND OUR CAPACITY TO THINK.
- EVERY LEADER IN EVERY CHURCH NEEDS TO COMMIT TO THIS.

- BEING WHOLEHEARTEDLY AND COMPLETELY COMMITTED TO THIS, SHOULD BE THE VISION OF EVERY CHRISTIAN IN EVERY CHURCH.
- EVERY MINISTRY NEEDS TO COMMIT TO THIS.
- EVERY ORGANISATION AND DENOMINATION NEED TO COMMIT TO THIS.
- THE EARLY APOSTLES AND SOME IN THE EARLY CHURCH WERE SO CONSUMED BY THIS THAT IT TOOK THEM AWAY FROM THEIR PROFESSION, THEIR WIVES, THEIR FAMILIES AND IN THE END, EVEN THEIR VERY LIVES.

Once we have accepted this, I believe we are then in the position for God to show us **our individual and specific role** in achieving this big vision. If spiritually, you are not in the position where God can give you your own specific vision for your life, then I believe He wants you to work with the vision of those He has put over you and with the vision of the church in which He has placed you. Do you know that fulfilling God's plans or purpose, or vision for your life is the most important thing you can ever do? This is the very reason why He created you in the first place. There is nothing more exciting or more fulfilling than this.

It is so important; Jesus says our very destiny depends on it. *"Not everyone that says unto me Lord, Lord shall enter into the Kingdom of Heaven, but* ***those that do the will (vision) of My Father."*** We need to know that God's purpose and plans (His vision) for our lives existed way before we came into the world. We were manifested to fulfil the vision that God had for us.

Accepting this, enlarges the boundaries of our minds and our thinking. It increases our capacity to receive and ultimately, to grow and to give. In the Gospel of John12:27 (KJV), Jesus, after realising that His hour had come, made an amazing statement that principally applies to every child of God. *"For this CAUSE (purpose) came I unto this hour".* This statement brings me to my final point.

DREAMS ARE FOR A SPECIFIC TIME

Because every dream or vision God gives is usually for a **specific time and place,** we must realise that they will not happen until we arrive at the **specific time, place and season.**

> God gave Joseph a vision in Canaan of being a world ruler, but *it could only be fulfilled in Egypt and at a particular time.*

Consequently, every dream has to go through a process, a trial if you please, and as a result, many things will come to try and distract you from your dreams.

"Indeed, I am against those who prophesy false dreams," declares the LORD. "They tell them and lead my people astray with their reckless lies, yet I did not send or appoint them. They do not benefit these people in the least," declares the LORD."

- Jeremiah 23:32 (KJV)

CHAPTER 15

DISTRACTERS TO YOUR DREAMS

It is not written in the Scriptures, but it is proven repeatedly by experience, that there will always be those whom you can call "dream stealers" or people who come to distract you from your dreams. They seem to come with the dreams as fruits come with a seed. Their one purpose will be to try and distract you from your dreams.

In Nehemiah chapter six, we have the interesting account of the rebuilding of the wall of Jerusalem by Nehemiah and the remnant who came back from the Babylonian captivity with him. This was part of the vision of Nehemiah for the restoration of Jerusalem. This was also God's will and purpose for the nation at that time. Was this going to happen trouble-free? Of course not! Doing God's work is rarely trouble-free. There are always distracters from fulfilling God's vision. And so, right on cue, came Sanballat and his friends, trying to distract Nehemiah and the children of Judah.

Nehemiah's response to this distraction should become the standard for everyone who wishes to be successful in fulfilling God's vision for their lives. *"And I sent messengers unto them, saying,* ***I am doing a great work, so that I cannot come down: why should the work cease, whilst I leave it, and come down to you****?"* Nehemiah 6:3(KJV). Paul, writing to the Corinthians about an opportunity God had opened up for him to minister said, *"Because a great door for effective work has opened to me, even though many oppose me."* 1 Corinthians 16:9 (KJV). God opened up a door but there were still those who opposed it.

Even the Lord Jesus, had to battle against distractions. The devil tried desperately hard to distract Him by offering what seemed like a much easier and more lucrative alternative route to getting the kingdom. But Jesus remained focused. The devil showed Him "all the kingdoms of this world in a moment of time and the glory of them." But He did not know that Jesus' kingdom was not of this world.

Sometimes, however, the distraction is self-inflicted. We can become our own distracters, by being overly preoccupied with things that do not relate to our vision.

Spending our time on trivialities and unimportant issues that add no value whatsoever. Distractions.... As soon as you have a dream, look for these also.

DISCOURAGERS OF YOUR DREAM

If you do not face distractions from your dreams, there are always things and those who will seek to discourage you. They are sent to you to dissuade and to dishearten. They will pop up from the most unlikely places as well. Sometimes it is the process you have to go through in moving towards your vision. This is challenging. In Numbers 21:4, the Bible says, the children of Israel were discouraged because of the way. Where were they going? To the land that God had promised them, to inherit the vision for the nation. So even the path you take towards your dream can be the very thing that discourages you.

Then, in Numbers chapter 13, we have the children of Israel coming right to the very threshold of their promise. This was the place that God had promised them four hundred years earlier. Now, here they were, standing on the very edge of that promise. The spies had returned with the evidence that the land was exactly as God had told them. Everyone should have been on cloud nine when they saw those huge bunches of grapes and the pomegranates.

Even the nations that were inhabiting the land were the ones whom God had told them would be living there. What could go wrong now? Would the Canaanites' enemy come to defeat them? No, it was not the Canaanites whom they needed to fear in this case - the enemies were right there amongst them. As I have said, discouragers can pop up from the most unlikely places. Who were they in this case? The very ones who had come back with evidence of the goodness of the land! These spies were standing there with the huge bunch of grapes and the pomegranates in their hand, confirming what God had told them. What a defining moment! On the very edge of their destiny, but they could not take a step further **because of the discouragers of their vision**. The discouragers did what the giant in the land or the Canaanites could not do. It defeated them on the very threshold of their destiny.

DECEIVERS OF YOUR DREAMS

Then, of course, there are sometimes deceivers who will try to deceive and prevent you from fulfilling your dreams. In Matthew 24:24 (KJV) Jesus, in teaching the disciples about the destruction of Jerusalem and His second coming, repeatedly warned His followers of false prophets and false teachers who would try to deceive them. Some seven times, He sandwiched this warning in His teaching to the disciples about this most important event. These deceivers would come to lead you away from your vision.

DESTROYERS OF YOUR VISION

Finally, the whole purpose of these distracters, discouragers, and deceivers is to try to do one thing. This thing is to destroy your dreams and visions. Oh, this would be a happy day for them, if they could do that! There is no clearer example than the life of the young man Joseph. Given these amazing dreams and visions for his life by God Himself, Joseph excitedly shared his visions with his brothers and his parents. The clear implications of these dreams challenged the very culture of how things were done at that time. Joseph, the youngest son, was seemingly going to be the ruler of the entire family, including his father and mother. How could this be? It was a challenge for both the parents and the brothers. His dreams were fundamentally counter to their cultural practices and norms.

Let me say here that not everyone will understand God's vision for your life; and dare I say it, sometimes not even those whom God has put over you to guide you. This does not mean that we should become proud and arrogant towards them and despise their leadership and guidance. Of course, this cannot be the way to act. No, we follow the example of our Lord Jesus. When at twelve, He felt He was ready to do His father's will, His parents corrected Him, but what did He do? The Bible says, He went back with them and submitted Himself to them. As I have said before, every vision is always for a specific time and a specific place. For the Scriptures tell us that years later, Jesus came preaching and the very first thing he declared was, *"**the time is fulfilled**, repent and believe the gospel."* His correct season had come.

As for Joseph, his dream stealers were his very own brothers who *"hated him yet the more because of his visions and dreams,"* the Bible says in Genesis 37:8 (KJV). When his father sent him to look after his brothers, the Bible reveals, *"But when they saw him in the distance, and before he reached them, they plotted to kill him. "Here comes that dreamer!"* they said to each other. *"Come now, let's kill him and throw him into one of these cisterns and say that a ferocious animal devoured him. Then we'll see what comes of his dreams."* Genesis 37: 18-20 (NIV)

What was the main thing that they hated about Joseph? It was his visions and dreams. You need to realise that many times when people hate you it is not just because of you. If you are a person of vision and have dreams that may seem to set you on a different trajectory from them, this can sometimes make them feel you are a threat to them, and so, they never feel comfortable with you because of your dreams. Never ever despise them or hate them. Like Joseph, who was shown that he would be the Saviour of the very brothers who hated him and the very parents who did not understand him, the salvation of your haters may be the very reason why God gave you your vision and your dreams. Think about that.

"When you believe in your dream and your vision, then it begins to attract its own resources. No one was born to be a failure."

— Myles Munroe

CHAPTER 16

DEATH, BURIAL AND THE RESURRECTION OF YOUR VISION

Some of us may escape the dream stealers, the deceivers, the discouragers, and the destroyers of our dreams, but all of us have to go through the next phase of our dreams. It is a phase that I once heard a very anointed preacher call, *"The death, the burial and the resurrection of a vision."* I have never forgotten that. Sometimes it could seem that our dream or our vision is completely dead.

Things haven't worked out as how you expected. So, it seems like there is no point in hoping and believing any longer. Can I tell you that this is the natural process for every single vision? This is the law of life and reproduction. Every seed has to go through death and burial, but when it is resurrected, then this is when God is ready for you. God taught this principle to the children of Israel. God gave promises to Abraham and Sarah, but waited until their bodies were dead, as it were.

- ✓ Moses knew that God was going to use him, but God waited until Moses thought it was too late.
- ✓ God showed which ministry He chose by causing Aaron's dead rod to bud and bear fruit.
- ✓ Jesus said, except a corn of wheat falls into the ground and dies, it abides alone, but if it dies, it bears MUCH FRUIT.

What do the Scriptures exhort us to do if the vision tarries? *"For the vision is yet for an appointed time, but at the end it shall speak, and not lie: though it tarry, wait for it; because it will surely come, it will not tarry."* Habakkuk 2:3 (KJV). And what shall we do in the meantime? *"Whatsoever you hand find to do, do it with all your heart."* Ecclesiastes 9:10 (KJV)

WE ARE THE CULMINATION OF GOD'S DREAM

Right now, there are millions of people all over the world, of every ethnicity, class, colour and creed who are called the "ekklesia," the church, the *called out* ones. They are called by the Lord Jesus out of this world's systems, this world's values and practices. They have believed on the Lord Jesus, in His death, burial and resurrection, as their substitute for their sins. Consequently, they have repented of their sins. They have been baptised in His amazing name. They have been born again by His Word and His Spirit, and they are seeking to live a holy life in this present world system, steadfastly looking for His glorious return.

Consequently, they are now called the sons and daughters of the Most High God. They believe implicitly that He will be returning one day to take them to live with Him forever. Here, He will create a new heaven and a new earth where there will be no more sin, sickness or suffering. There will only be righteousness and the love of God, all because before the foundation of the world, GOD HIMSELF HAD A DREAM. A dream of having a Kingdom of sons and daughters, made in His image and likeness. A people who would demonstrate His love and character to the entire universe. A people who were going to eventually become His bride. He gave us a glimpse of this in the way He created Eve for Adam. He was put to sleep and out of his body, the Lord God took a rib and built it into a woman, then came and presented her to Adam. Paul teaches that Adam was a type of Christ.

The Lord did not just go to sleep, but He gave His very life when he was crucified on the cross. As a result, out of Him came the Holy Spirit who has baptised us into one body and is now making us into the Bride of Christ! And guess what? One day very soon, He will be returning to take His church home, to see the fulfilment of His dream, His glorious vision.

This was God's vision, His dream for His church. He has not given up on His dream despite all that has taken place in human history. Despite all that the devil is always trying to destroy God's vision. The Word of God said, *"He shall see the travail of His soul and be satisfied."* Isaiah 53:11 (KJV)

In the Book of Revelation, the Apostle John was given a picture of the perfected Bride of Christ, the fulfilled vision of our amazing Lord.

- *One of the seven angels who had the seven bowls full of the seven last plagues came and said to me, "Come, I will show you the bride, the wife of the Lamb." Rev. 21:9 (KJV)*
- *Now I saw a new heaven and a new earth, for the first heaven and the first earth had passed away. Also there was no more sea. 2 Then I, John, saw the holy city, New Jerusalem, coming down out of heaven from God, prepared as a bride adorned for her husband. 3 And I heard a loud voice from*

> *heaven saying, "Behold, the tabernacle of God is with men, and He will dwell with them, and they shall be His people. God Himself will be with them and be their God. 4 And God will wipe away every tear from their eyes; there shall be no more death, nor sorrow, nor crying. There shall be no more pain, for the former things have passed away. "Then He who sat on the throne said, "Behold, I make all things new." And He said to me, "Write, for these words are true and faithful. "And He said to me, "It is done! I am the Alpha and the Omega, the Beginning and the End. I will give of the fountain of the water of life freely to him who thirsts. 7 He who overcomes shall inherit all things, and I will be his God and he shall be My son.* Revelation 21:1-7 (KJV)

So, our amazing Lord Jesus also had to go through the death, the burial and the resurrection of His dream…but even though it seems as if His dream is tarrying, it will come.

Exertion without a vision leads to exhaustion. Exertion with a vision produces inspiration.

- *Emile Austin*

CHAPTER 17

CONCLUSION

So, we have looked at the power of having a vision or dream for our lives. We have seen that it is one of the most powerful and life transforming blessings that God could ever bestow upon an individual. He has, in fact, invested your purpose and your destiny in that seed of a dream He has placed in your spirit. These dreams and visions have also consistently proven to be the greatest producer of wealth and prosperity from the most unlikely sources. As we have said, every discovery, and every invention that has transformed this world of ours, all came from a vision, a dream.

Never again therefore must we look at ourselves, or the contribution we can make, as insignificant. The God Who designed us is the One Who defines who we are, and what we are capable of. So, despite all that has been achieved so far, there is still a slot in God's plan for you and your ideas, your visions, and your dreams. Your world will not be impacted or improved without them. It does not matter the size of your vision. There are some seeds that are so small that they are no bigger than a speck of dust-like a particular species of the orchid plant. Yet it belongs to the second largest flowering plant family! Then there is the largest known seed, which is the Coco de Mer, the seed of a palm tree.

This seed can reach up to thirty centimetres long and weigh up to eighteen kilograms. Both make their unique contribution to nature, despite being so completely different in size. Yet, if we were to only go by their appearance in seed form, we would conclude, that poor, insignificant-looking Orchid had no place in the grand scheme of things. As we have established, like all seeds that we plant, our visions are given to us to bear fruit in their correct season. God in His sovereignty and wisdom has constructed this world with your slot carefully marked out for you. He now wants you to step into it.

I am always left speechless whenever I think about the amazing wisdom of God. When you think about all the amazing discoveries that man has made throughout the ages, in the areas of engineering, science, physics, electronics and now the computer and biotechnology. All of this knowledge was there from the very beginning when God created the universe in the Book of Genesis.

However, for thousands of years, the world did not benefit from any of these discoveries that we now enjoy, because it was not the correct season for the right people with the visions and dreams to come along and discover them. As the wise man Solomon said, *"To everything, there is a season and a time for every purpose under the sun." Ecclesiastes 3:1KJV* So let us continue to dream, to have visions, whatever their size. Be it the size of the seemingly insignificant orchid, or the size of the proud palm, your contribution will be equally amazing.

That Jesus should choose poor and ignorant fishermen to be His disciples and change the entire history of mankind is enough inspiration to believe that we too are called to make a difference. God's intention is to make this world of ours a much better place because of the visions and dreams He has placed in the hearts of people who seem to have nothing more than their visions and dreams.

So, there are no longer any justified excuses for us to continue to live unfulfilled lives. Some of the saddest pages in the Bible are those that simply mention the names of people who have existed but tell us nothing about their contribution to life. As we have said before, God has placed within each vision enough resources to service each vision. God Himself will see that if we work with Him and trust Him. He Himself will bring those dreams to pass. So, I urge you to keep dreaming. Keep having visions. They are God's special gifts to you and to His broken world.

References

1. Washington, Booker T. (1901). *The Story of My Life and Work: An Autobiography.* ISBN 978-3849674748. Archived from the original on April 6, 2023. Retrieved March 7, 2023.
2. Williams, Greg von. *Visionary Leadership.* https://www.linkedin.com/pulse/visionary-leadership-greg-von-williams. Published December 13, 2022.

Note:

All Scriptures are taken from the *Amplified Version, Berean Standard, Kings James, New Kings James* and *New International* Versions of *The Holy Bible.*

My Dreams and Visions Board

"Then the LORD replied: "Write down the revelation and make it plain on tablets so that a herald may run with it".

Habakkuk 2:2 (NIV)

My Dreams

My Visions

Tracking Your Dreams & Visions

Printed in Great Britain
by Amazon

46660516R00069